I AM with You

Poems Inspired by God

KAREN J CHISHOLM

Copyright © 2023 Karen J Chisholm

All rights reserved. No part of this book may be reproduced, stored, or transmitted by any means—whether auditory, graphic, mechanical, or electronic—without written permission of both publisher and author, except in the case of brief excerpts used in critical articles and reviews. Unauthorized reproduction of any part of this work is illegal and is punishable by law.

All images were created for and are the property of Karen J Chisholm.

All scripture quotations, unless otherwise indicated, are taken from the King James Version of the Bible.

Library of Congress Control Number: 2014915652

ISBN: 979-8-89031-426-0 (sc)
ISBN: 979-8-89031-427-7 (hc)
ISBN: 979-8-89031-428-4 (e)

Because of the dynamic nature of the Internet, any web addresses or links contained in this book may have changed since publication and may no longer be valid. The views expressed in this work are solely those of the author and do not necessarily reflect the views of the publisher, and the publisher hereby disclaims any responsibility for them.

One Galleria Blvd., Suite 1900, Metairie, LA 70001
(504) 702-6708
1-888-421-2397

This book is dedicated to the Glory of God

with special thanks to:

my mother, Genevieve Patterson:
You always tell me, "Go for it!"

and

my teacher, Gilda Roitman:
Because you believed I could, I believed I could.
You praised my eighth-grade efforts and planted a dream.

Contents

Section I: God Speaking

I AM with You 3
Praise Is 6
Do You Love Me? 8
In Me 11
I AM Peace 13
Presence 15
Live in God 20
Your Life is a Prayer 22
Forever Mine 24
You Want What I Want 28
Love 29
My Heart 32
Great Favor 34
Hear Me Louder – You Are Loved 35
Stay the Course 37
A Husband 39
Trial of Faith 40

Section II: Me Speaking To God

Shine 43
Doubts 46
You Pick Me Up 49
When I Am Weak and Found Wanting 53
Jealous for God 55

Great Things	58
Being Fully Present	60
Walk in the Light	62
Breakthrough!	65
No Condemnation	67
How Will I Know It's You?	69
Perceiving	70
My Offering	74
Awesome	75
Holy, Yet . . .	77

Section III: Me Speaking To Others

Fear	83
Music!	84
My Hand	86
The Same Man	88
Trust	89
Forgive Me	90
The Peace of God	92
Wishes	95

Section IV: Author

About the Author	99

Preface

These poems aren't perfect.
They are honest. They are real.
They are what they are.
Let them be a teaching tool.
Let them be a cause for prayer.
Let Christ be formed in you
As you receive the intent.
Let God's voice speak these words to your heart.
Let Holy Spirit lead you into truth as you think about
a word or a phrase that stands out to you.
If something bothers you, look up scripture to
prove these words line up with the Bible.
And enjoy.

These poems are God's gift to me in my morning quiet time, and I make of them a gift to you. I am so often amazed at the words that appear on the page as I write. I know these thoughts are not the ones I am used to living with day to day, and I worship God for His Truth revealed through me, a simple seeker who loves Him.

In these pages you will hear God speaking to you. You will also hear me whining at God (seems like when my writing is all about me and my shortcomings, I must be whining). And there follows a section that is perhaps rhetorical, perhaps not. We can all learn from the things written here. May these simple, sometimes inconsistent, poems bless you and draw you closer to Him.

Section I

GOD SPEAKING

I AM with You

All is well, Child. All is well
Mercy has overtaken you
Grace found you where you fell
Love has bound your wounds
Peace now lingers, covers all
And calm remains.

Always I AM with you
Whether sun or storm, grief and loss
Or times of joy and gladness
In tortures or in smiles
Through danger, fear, and trials
I AM
with you.

You have many questions
Think "If I just knew why"
Answers, though, are silent
Your heart pleads toward the sky
And I
AM with you.

Karen J Chisholm

You want justice to be known
Your innocence exclaim
What you get is accusation
Heaviness of blame
And I AM
with you.

Long you fought to make wrong right
Far you've come in vain
Misunderstood, cast to the night
Stand cold there in the rain
And I AM
with you.

Broken, bleeding, dying trying
Face calamity
End of hope and end of strength
Resigned you'll not be free
And I
AM with you.

Long the trying of your faith
Proclaims "Abandoned!" clear
And you accept in agony
This life of death drawn near
I AM
with you.

The trial long, how can you last
Existing just to breathe?
Decision died in hopelessness
Or hope deferred, time-wreathed
I AM
with you.

When, in time, the scars are old
And life grows loose in flesh
The fire-tried faith is strongest, most
The Spirit calm and fresh
And we
are One.

Welcome home.

Karen J Chisholm

Praise Is

Praise is not choosing the right words
Praise is an attitude

It is time you spend and the look on your face
When you think about Me
And how much you love Me

Praise is your sacrifice of time to be with Me
It is every thought you have of Me
And giving thanks

Praise is being thankful – Eucharisteo
Thanking Me in all things
Is music offered to Me that you cannot hear

Praise is telling Me who you think I am
Praise is seeking Me
It is offering yourself to Me

And how I cherish your offering and laudation!

I receive praise as you run to Me in trouble
I feel your praise
As you choose not to fear the future

My praise is perfected in you
As you look for good to follow trial

You are My praise
My Beloved
Adored

Praise often and freely
No words are required

A thankful heart shouts praise perfectly
I receive your praise as treasure

And from praise, I make your crown.

Karen J Chisholm

Do You Love Me?

Do you love without condition?
Can you reach out without wishin'
I would give you all the things
Your eyes see and you desire?

Could you come to Me in simplicity?
Would you take My Word and visit Me,
Come and spend time in My Presence,
Let us talk and laugh a while?

Remember when we met back in
The simple days of wonder
When you talked and I would listen
And you heard Me when I smiled?

Weren't we happy and carefree then
Without pretense, fear or life plan
When we teased and tried, we joked, we cried,
In short, we learned each other well?

Have you grown up, out, or old?
How did your love grow cold?
When did all the sweet, dear things
Lose importance, then take wings?

I AM with You

Do you ever stop and wonder
Just where the magic went?
Oh, I miss you and I love you
And I want no one above you.

If I could spend time with you walking,
Sometimes laughing, sometimes talking,
We could learn to know each other once again.

There is no one I desire
Just the way that I want you.
There is no one who can fill your place with Me.
I can love you when you don't love.
I can meet you on your own.

I will lift you ever higher;
As you praise Me, I'll send power
'Til we both can soar together
O'er the shadows of the day.

KAREN J CHISHOLM

Come and love Me, My Beloved,
Come and run with Me together.
Let us live and love and laugh and sing
And shout the victory!

For your praises bring Me closer
And your joy comes overflowing
When delights of love fulfill us
As you revel in My grace.

And your spirit soars with Mine now
While the world is left behind now
And "phileo" becomes "agape"
'Cause your spirit's finally free!

Soar with Me!
In victory!
Be set free!
Just stay with Me!

In Me

Every day new life is cast,
Each day different than the last.
Some grow closer to Me still,
Some draw back, won't let Me fill.

Come and try Me. Come and see.
I reward all who seek Me.
I AM with you, though unseen.
I'm the one who makes you clean.

You want more than what you have.
I would lead you on My path.
When you hesitate and seek,
I will find you, I AM meek.

Come and sup and stay a while.
I will fill you, make you smile.
You will stretch, lean in to Me
And My Spirit make you free.

You'll return into your day
Refreshed, revived, walk on your way.
Peace inside you'll carry, too,
Knowing I've spent time with you.

Come back often, come back soon.
Fellowship that dispels gloom
Fills you up with joy inside.
Holy Spirit 'comes your guide.

And you'll find with peace you go
Into new life with My glow.
Others notice, turn aside,
See My Spirit, Love abide

On you . . . in Me.

I AM Peace

Why do you look for Me
When I AM here beside you?
Why do you search and stumble
While I want to guide you?

If you stop and give it up now,
All to Jesus you surrender,
You will find Me, for I'm with you.
You'll find love and you'll find truth.
You'll find Me.

I AM peace no man can fathom;
I AM peace.
I can satisfy you fully,
But My price is full surrender.
Here with Jesus I AM always;
I AM peace.

All the places you've been looking,
All the plans you've made in vain,
All the ways you've tried to catch Me,
All the times you've feigned to have Me,
Have been wasted 'til you stop
And let Me win.

Karen J Chisholm

For with Jesus' love you'll find Me.
There's no other way to have Me.
Jesus loves you;
Open now and let Him in.

If you reach for, grasp for, work for
Peace, you won't obtain it.
Peace overtakes you only when
You stand still.

I AM with You

Presence

All the day I'm close beside you
Every way I'm teaching you.
All that happens in your life here
I will use to shape you too.

I'm the Potter; I AM shaping
From inside to look like Me.
When your inner core is transformed,
Thoughts and actions become free:

Free to love because I love you,
Free to smile and to agree,
Focused on your heavenly Father,
You begin to sound like Me.

Things around you take on new life,
People want to be with you.
You feel light, feel joy and laughter.
Nothing's heavy; all feels new.

You will know you've been empowered,
Ready, tackle any chore.
New awareness of surroundings,
Loving people even more.

Sometimes felt, this joy inside you
Means you've focused here on Me.
Means My Presence fills and guides you
Connected to the Holy Three
Who are One.

KAREN J CHISHOLM

This is place you wish to stay in;
This is where My power swells.
This I offer every day in
This place holds salvation's wells.

Joy abundant offered freely
To all those who draw this water.
Spending time, stay focused on Me
Welcome every son and daughter.

Here you draw My joy abundant.
Here rejoice and worship true.
This, your source of strength and power
To face day's assaults on you.

Ever holding hands with Me,
You can dance and laugh with joy,
See more clearly what's before you
As you walk, My sight employ.

Then you better love your brother,
Fend off word darts hurled at you.
Not so often take offense,
Find loving others easier too.

How to get there every day,
To these wells I'm speaking of?
Being thankful in all trials
Keeps you covered in My Love.

I AM with You

Attitude is lighter, dearer
As you focus just on Me,
See as I see, it comes clearer
Thoughts, more positive you'll be.

So the secret is My Presence,
Staying open just to Me,
Focused on My holiness, and
Less aware yourself, 'come free.

Walking in the Light revealed you,
Leaning on Me, taking flight.
Then the mundane parts of living
Become joy and work seems light.

Now when others share successes
You'll rejoice with them and smile,
For My Presence through your messes
Kept you positive the while.

And the joy of your salvation,
Close relationship with Me,
Bought through Christ blood invitation:
Whosoever will be free.

It takes practice, daily striving
Against sin, focused on Me,
Batting thoughts back to the sly one,
Your mind, holy, can be free.

Karen J Chisholm

Giving thanks and thinking higher,
Not entangled this world's draw,
As you talk with people you meet,
You won't flinch from their words raw.

As they complain and you stay thankful,
They'll be drawn or walk away.
Filled with Light, you are My witness;
Your words, praise filled, woo or flay.

All will answer when time's over
For each word they've uttered here.
Let your words reveal your faith.
While speak of weather, yet can cheer.

Bringing hope to those found seeking,
Giving opportunity,
They may ask for soul direction;
You can direct them Me.

Now your query has been answered.
Positive your life can be.
Walk in Light with burdens lifted,
Possible when you're in Me.

I AM with You

How to get there: daily focus,
Time with Me in Word and prayer.
Listening Spirit's direction,
Ministering words I share.

Carry on, Beloved Pilgrim.
You keep walking; I will guide.
Always knowing I AM with you,
More aware I'm at your side.

You become more used to seeing
Things the way I show to you.
Stumble maybe, but recover,
Hold more tightly, see what's true.

I AM leading to new vistas
While your feet are on the ground.
This becomes My tested servant,
Meeting each day without frown.

Just thankful . . . for Presence

KAREN J CHISHOLM

Live in God

Don't look back – I'm not there.
Look at Me, let go of fear.
Don't look ahead – it isn't time
To face that day, to start that climb.

But look at now while it is here,
Commune with Me while I AM near
And let Me do this work in you;
Hold still and let Me make you new.

You need My strength, so take My joy
And cast down fear – My name employ.
Let My Spirit fight the foe,
Already done when you let go.

Just step aside and see My might.
Allow My way to end the fight
And spend your time just praising Me,
Then look around; you've been set free!

But keep your eyes and guard your sight,
Stay in My word, refuse the flight
That self suggests in whelming odds,
For you are safe; you're hid in God!

List no longer to the enemy.
Hear only My voice; let Me lead.
And know your steps are ordered o'er;
Believe 'tis God who opens doors.

And rest in Me, My Spirit dwells
In those who trust and those who tell
The way that I work in your life,
The times I've met and ended strife.

And tell of Jesus' life lain down
And bear the cross that earns a crown.
For when this timid life is past,
You'll be with Me at long, long last!

Karen J Chisholm

Your Life is a Prayer

Every day you talk to Me
In simple ways others don't see.
My word in you comes from your mouth
Encouraged, remembering I brought you out.

Always see good, expecting by faith,
I receive glory through life lived in grace.
Pray never knowing the outcome, but trust
Time will reveal, so pray on as you must.

Resisting the enemy, in faith stand firm
Though darts pierce deeply to see if you'll squirm.
But you shake them off, saying,
"I trust you, Jesus."
You keep on going. This is what pleases.

You've learned to accept,
When you're wrong, make amends,
Ask forgiveness, forgiving,
Suffering long to life's end

All the tedious tasks entrusted to you,
Waiting patient in work I've given to do.
Believing the time that you've given to Me
More precious than all that needs doing you see.

Investing life talents entrusted to you,
Believing God's purpose,
Plan, will carried through.

I AM with You

You understand it may all come to nothing,
Are willing to sit here with Me – just listening
That act alone has a crown waiting for you.
Few others see, understand this as you do.

I AM filling you, drenching your soul.
With life dew of heaven, I'm filling your bowl.
As you spend time with Me simply wearing out pencil,
I'm saving souls through these words time will stencil.

In heaven your songs are treasured and stored
And all of your poems, each jot, tittle, word,
Each lyric and line, each subtle erasure
Are watched and are weighted by God's own nature.

As you draw daily these words Spirit guides,
Father God smiles, Jesus glorified.
And all will be known the way you intended
When motives are bared as all time has ended.

So just keep on writing while there is time
For this is oasis in life path you climb.
And these words are sustenance in days to come.
You've yet much to go through 'fore death you succumb.

And I AM your Father, your Maker, your Guide;
Great Three-in-One God who deals with your pride,

Reveals how to die to self daily to win
Life's greatest rewards there secreted within
You . . .
My treasure
My delight
My own

Karen J Chisholm

Forever Mine

Beloved, you are precious to Me.
You are well adored.
You will see Me as I AM

You feel My Presence
In the breeze feel My caress
More aware each day of Me
My Presence everywhere

You reach out; you look up
I your life have filled
Life well lived and time well spent
Satisfied you dwell

Daughter One, you are well loved
I AM yours and you are Mine
Only God, Beloved Friend
True worshipper I find

Ask Me anything you want
I will satisfy
You're My treasure, well begot
Your life, your reins I've tried

I've found you faithful
Quick repenter
Crying o'er what hurts My heart
Willing servant, unrelenter
Giving all to make new start

I AM with You

You are Mine. You offer freely,
Give your life My plans fulfill
Listen closely, write My words down
Every day you listen, still

Where else can I find a writer
One who lets Me have full sway?
There are many, each one special
None like you, though, Special K.

Named you Karen – I love that name
Carin' is what you do best
Loving Me is all I ask for
You do it well; I do the rest.

Soon I'm coming back to get you
I'll receive you to myself
Every groan and tear have mattered
Every sigh I've treasured well

Keep on coming, walking toward Me
I will help along the way
Keep on working through the nighttime
I'll reward when it is Day

What I like, though,
What touches Me is
You don't care if I reward
You just want to be here with Me
You adore and are adored

Karen J Chisholm

Child, no matter what I give you
You try hard, you give your best
I inhabit all your praises
I AM in you – perfect rest.

Just know
You are
Loved.

I don't care how you smell
I don't care what you wear
I love what's inside you
Where My Spirit dwells.

Come unto Me
I come to you
Touching the throne
Your words rise to Me

Tell unto others
All that I give you
My words accomplish
They set lost souls free

Write when I tell you
Listen to Me
Dance in My Presence
Beloved, you're free!

Can I have You, God?

You have Me.
Every moment
Everywhere
Every day, second, minute, hour
Everywhere in or out of time
I delight in all you're doing
Only know I call you Mine.

You are Mine
Forever
Mine

Karen J Chisholm

You Want What I Want

Daughter One, you are so precious to Me.
You want what I want: souls saved.
You pray and ask and feel the need
And pray and ask some more.

You pray for strangers in their cars
As you follow them down the freeway.
You pray for people in ambulances
When you hear sirens going by,

Asking Me to give them
One more chance for salvation,
Asking Me to put praying EMTs with them
And reaching out with your spirit to their spirit to help.

You want what I want: for all to be saved.

Keep on doing what I give you to do.
Don't worry over what doesn't get done.
I AM with you.
My angels run to do My will, answering your prayers.
I AM with you and you are loved.

Love

It's under the Blood. I see you perfect.
I know your struggles. I feel your pain.
I'm there in trials. I give you comfort
And strength to stand, begin again.

I'm with you always. You're Mine alone.
Through every heartbreak, I'm still the One
Who holds and comforts, who stands beside.
I AM your comfort, your Friend and Guide.

You think you can't stop
Knocking your head against a brick wall.
Use your weapons;
That wall will fall.

I have equipped you to stand and win.
You see yourself weak, victim again.
The truth is, I have conquered for you.
Stand and deliver: My Word, My Truth.

My Word is more than just your sword.
My power through you strikes a chord
And light will shine in darkness when
You speak My Word, let it defend.

The truth may hurt a little while
But clears the air and brings a smile.
When both agree that I AM right,
Then both surrender; that ends the fight.

Lift your eyes off of yourself.
Do not find fault, self to defend.
Take no offense when words are spoken
And there will be no bridge to mend.

Always love. Love keeps no score.
Words roll off love and out the door.
Love looks for good, ignores the rest.
Love yourself first. That's the true test.

When you love yourself,
You have love to give.
When your need is met,
You can be generous.

Be happy in yourself
And it will not matter where you are.
When you love yourself,
No one else is required to meet your needs.

To love yourself, you must forgive,
Accept, bless, love, nurture.
Refuse to give others power to hurt you.
Refuse to look for flaws in yourself
And you won't notice flaws in others.
Be good to yourself and you'll be good to others.
Start with you.

If you love yourself, you won't lie to yourself,
You won't keep things from yourself,
You won't punish yourself.
You will reward yourself with good things.
You will have a generous spirit.
You will live free.

Begin now.
Accept yourself as you are.
See yourself as perfect,
Needing no change in weight
Or hair or clothes or home or car.
Accept what is.
Value what is.
Embrace what is.
Love.

My Heart

Into My heart
Bring your tears and your pain;
I'll cover and hover
And bring joy again.

Come quickly, believe
Spirit's sword from your knees.
Swing boldly, arc high;
Reach right up to the sky.

Forever I'll claim you;
I made you, I named you.
Testify, overcome
By the blood of My Son.

Tell My great acts
And of spirit-felt moments.
Write of My ardor
In ways Spirit foments.

Come often,
Spend time
Long or short
As you climb

Through life.

I AM with You

Do it for Me;
Want to be free.
Do it for you
And I'll see you through.

Believe Me for big things,
Trust Me more and more.
I'll open, none shutting,
Each window and door.

Go through them believing
I'm leading this way.
I'm not disappointed;
I'm with you this day.

My heart overflows
With the love that I show
Through frail vessels like you
Born again, born anew.

You, My daughters and sons
Each with Me now begun,
You have all touched My heart;
Yes, you did from the start.

Remember My Son.
He is Lord, Holy One.
And He . . .
Is My Heart.

Karen J Chisholm

Great Favor

Daughter, you are loved with an everlasting Love.
There has never been, nor will there ever be
A time you could possibly be alone,
For I AM with you.

I have given you favor among men (mankind).
You are Mine.
You have great favor with Me.
Great favor with Me.

You are precious and beloved and treasured.
You are special to Me.
You are set apart for My service, dedicated to Me alone.

Beloved.
Complete in Christ.
Equipped.
Adorned with and by Holy Spirit.

You are Mine, Daughter, you are Mine.
Go and do My will today, Child.
Ask Holy Spirit to control your mind,
And go in peace

And in
Great Favor.

Hear Me Louder – You Are Loved

Hear Me, Child.
Hear Me louder.
You are loved.
You are truly, completely, wonderfully, *completely* LOVED!
There is a reason you are being told this repeatedly, over and over.
Hear Me, Child, you are *loved*.

In order to come deeper with Me,
You must *believe* you are loved
And you do not yet accept it,
Comprehend the truth of it,
Believe it in your deepest, inmost being.

When you understand what I AM telling you,
What My Spirit is saying to you,
And you *know* that you know that you know you are loved,
You will begin to love yourself unconditionally and well.

When you are able to do that, your life will change.
You will change.
How you connect with people will change.

Then you will love unconditionally, without price,
Fully loving and accepting people.
Then you will be loved and sought out and wanted.
When you believe I love you,
You will finally be able to receive the love of people.
You will be healed.

Karen J Chisholm

And, so, you will begin to live
The abundant life I have prepared for you.
You will receive the money and possessions
I alone can give.
It is your call. Let Me know.

Let Me know that you hear Me.
I am filling you with Me.
You will give out and give out
And never be depleted, never tire.
You will be free.

Begin now.
Love Me with supernatural ability,
For I have granted that unto you.

Love Me completely.
Love Me unreservedly.
Love Me loved.
My Beloved, love Me.

I send you out to absolutely love Me.
Continue in My Love, My Beloved.
You do well.

Take your rest now
Soon you will rise
To love
Me.

I AM with You

Stay the Course

Daughter, you are feeling
You don't know what to do next.
Pray.

When you don't know what to do next, pray.
When you don't have clear direction, stay.
When you know you have My answer, obey.
It really is that simple.

When you're doing all you can and it is hard, pray.
When you're done and given up hope, stay.
When I give you clear direction, obey.
Just take a step; I am with you.

For each dream you've given up on, I've been there.
Every time you beat yourself up,
I've been with you through despair.
Then you hear a word of hope
And you see you *can* succeed.
So you start again, then falter,
But there's something you don't see:

You've come farther down the path.
You've learned things you didn't know.
And you've encouraged others,
'Specially those who are going slow.
And if you ask for help, then do what you've been told,
There's nothing that can stop or keep you
From reaching every goal.

Karen J Chisholm

It's you.
The hurdle you must cross,
The lake to get around,
The mountain in your way,
The muddy, shaky ground
Are all to make you stronger
And are just part of the course.
So let go of the fear and doubt
And scuttle old remorse.

Just look for Me. I AM your Guide.
Reach out your hand; place it in Mine.
Then keep your eyes focused on Me,
Not on the path, and soon you'll see . . .
You're there.

Step by step.
Line by line.
Precept upon precept.

Stay the course.

I AM with You

A Husband

Don't pray for God to give you a husband;
Pray for God to present you as a gift of God
To the man He chooses.

Do for your husband what you want him to do for you;
He is your closest neighbor.
When you love your husband this way, you please God,
Your husband doesn't feel judged by you,
And you have peace.

Holy Spirit

Karen J Chisholm

Trial of Faith . . .

A Word from the Lord

I didn't give you a feel-good faith.
I called you to take up your cross and follow Me.
Remember, as Christ did, the joy set before you.
Worship, as Job did, the God who does not explain.
Keep yourself by My Word. My joy is your strength.
I have brought you by the path that brings Me glory.
Small trials, small faith, small glory.
I will not be confined to small faith.
I AM.
My will be done.
In you.
By you.
For you.
To you.
My grace is sufficient for this trial of your faith.
My glory rests on you.
When you praise Me because I AM . . .
Because in My wisdom
I place you in situations not your choosing . . .
And worship . . .
I AM glorified.

Section II

ME SPEAKING TO GOD

I AM with You

Shine

Lord, here I am in my little world;
All I see here is about me.
Impatience, anger are quick to rise
For others, self in what I see.

This is wearing; life seems flat.
Unrewarding days are mine.
Then something different I perceive:
A little glimmer starts to shine.

I begin to come aware
That all I do and am comes short
And I can't fix my faults myself
Or change my ways; I'm out of sorts.

I am looking all around
And I am restless; nothing suits.
The things that used to bring me pleasure
Now fall flat to boot.

And I don't like me anymore.
All's out of control.
Yeah, I've always known of You.
I see now I'm not whole.

I need *something* . . .

Then Your Light begins to shine
In places I want dark.
I don't want to talk about
The things that bear shame's mark.

Karen J Chisholm

Light of Your Presence shines so hard
On what I thought was hid,
And guilt is heavy, weighs me down,
I'm shamed by all I did.

I can't escape and I can't stop
Remembering this stuff.
And I agree I'm sinner sure
Then You say, "It's enough."

So I ask Jesus to forgive,
To come live in my heart.
I'm given faith, begin belief,
You give me fresh new start!

I feel the burden roll away
Of wrongs I can't make right.
The darkness flees and I can see
I stand now in Your Light.

You love me. Dare I trust that thought?
I've nothing good to give.
Cheater, thief, manipulator,
Don't deserve to live.

Yet You console and make me whole;
New hope You've put inside.
Love me as I am, You said,
The old me now has died.

I AM with You

But it keeps trying to arise;
Your Word keeps me on keel.
Scripture more I memorize,
More peace I then can feel.

I make mistakes and I offend;
You love me just the same.
So I begin to trust You when
You say for sin You came.

'Cause sin I've got a plenty of
Yet pleased with me You dwell.
How can that be? And yet it is,
So I begin to tell.

All who'll listen, I would speak:
I'm free and happy now!
You can be too if only you
Come meet Savior I've found.

Old friends now don't come around.
I wonder, is it me?
Or is it that You shine Your Light
And too their sin they see?

Lord, shine through me
'Til all can see
Only You
And be born too . . . new

To Shine.

Karen J Chisholm

Doubts

Lord, I come to You in Jesus' name.
Help me come to You, Lord.
Help me find my way.

Every time I'm so unsure,
Embarrassed I would say
To come in disarray
This way.

I'm not so neat or polished, Lord,
Have trouble finding words.
Unsure and I don't understand
But still afraid You've heard.

And yet my need compels me sure
To seek You anyway.
No one else can bring me peace
Like Your words will today.

But will You speak or silent be?
How can I know for sure?
Are You there but I cannot hear
Through pain I can't endure?

So I come boldly anyway.
Then, knowing I'm not good,
I stop in fear, but then proceed
On faith legs made of wood.

I AM with You

Have mercy on me, a sinner.
My pride won't let me bow.
I'm so ashamed and in such pain,
Unworthy anyhow

Of notice by the God of Heaven,
But I have heard of grace.
So I am hoping You'll have pity,
Just a crumb I'll taste.

An answer not for me but one
Who never had the chance
To laugh and run and feel the sun,
To hop and skip and dance.

Have mercy.
Deliver.
Heal.
The innocent.
And I will bear my sin.
And go.
Away.

But I come to You and You hear me:
Words from lips unclean
And hearing, answer not just petition
But I know that You've seen

My heart black and hopeless.
Yet You smiled on me
And let me know I'm loved the same
As one so innocent,
Accepted here just as I am:

Scarred.

Karen J Chisholm

How can You just accept me now?
You know what I have done.
You'd really take me? Let me know You?
That's too simple.

I can't live a perfect life.
You know once I tried.
But then I lost the one I love
And something's broke inside.

And I'm not young and gullible,
I'm tough and I'll be fine.
And yet there's something about You
I thought I'd never find:
Peace.

I could use some peace right now
'Cause things have gone all wrong.
And I don't like what life's become
And find I'm not that strong.

So I'm listening.
If You can move mountains,
Move me.

Prove You won't leave me too.

Why should I give up my freedom
Just to come serve You?
Anyway.

You Pick Me Up

Lord, thank You.
You are with me.
Always.

I can be hard on myself.
You keep on encouraging.
Like a crawling infant on the floor
Who wants to run
But is only pulling up,
I often fall.

Often.

Fall.

Often.

And when I do . . . You pick me up.

You encourage me.
When I complain
And sometimes whine,
You rephrase
In positive ways
And say, "You're fine! You're Mine."
You pick me up.

When I'm depressed
And I just eat,
You bid me come
Sit at Your feet,
Then talk of all
You have for me,
And how I please You,
How You see
Me perfect.

And focused on You
Instead of me,
Forget my pain.
I laugh; I'm free,
And marvel there
Right in my chair
How
You pick me up.

When I'm o'erwhelmed
And deadline looms,
Go without sleep
'Til finish blooms
You stay right there with me,
Guiding me,
Giving strength,
Unheard; I see

While thanking You
It's done at last,
I take deep breath,
So glad it's past.

I AM with You

And in my checking
Each detail,
I realize
That without fail
You helped,
Encouraged to complete,
Choose better word,
Edit, delete,
And add detail
Until it's done.
On time.
You pick me up.

When my life
Is done at last
And as I'm going,
My eyes cast
For You, my Friend,
Who loved me best,
Are with me
As I move
From past to Presence,
From work to joy,
From life's temptation,
To heaven's foundation.

And I can see
As faith has grown
So many times
I'd've given up alone
But trusted yet
The One I love.

Karen J Chisholm

You pick me up
Like date at door
And take me
To that distant shore.
Like bride at lintel,
Cross threshold
Held.

Once more . . .
. . . You pick me up.

I AM with You

When I Am Weak and Found Wanting

When I am weak and found wanting,
When I am helpless to change,
I long for Your arms, for Your soothing voice,
For Your calm assurance that I am.

You show me Your view and I forget all around me
Look up, and I see all the blessings You've made
Spending time in Your arms
Changes the way I see everything.

Nothing can stop me or claim me or keep me
In Your arms I am strong, unafraid, know my rights
Then step out on my own with You deep inside
. . . and I am.

When I have been in Your Presence,
All around me is less.
Less important, less pressing,
Less confusion, less mess.

Christ in me! Formed by faith!
Belief in action, not playing safe.
I can do all as You work through me.
At Your call, I am, I see.

KAREN J CHISHOLM

When I believe
And I know Your will,
I stand alone,
Keep standing still

'Til all is done
'Til all is won
'Til victory is mine
And glory God's.

My Father, my Brother, My Friend, and my Comforter,
My King and my Lord And my Holy Redeemer.

You ARE . . .
. . . and I am.

I AM with You

Jealous for God

Am I jealous for You, God?
Fight for what's yours?
What does that look like?
How can I be sure?

Do I walk away
From the things of this world
That trap and entangle
And 'round me are curled?

If I focus on them,
They then hold me fast.
I must focus on You
'Til their lure has passed.

The treasures of this life
Can pass in a day,
The treasures of heaven
Are mine for alway.

And so the eternal
Unseen, yet exists,
Has value unweighed here,
Unfelt through the mists.

But more real than skin-pinch,
Eternity's core;
God's promises ready
Are now held in store

KAREN J CHISHOLM

Until time is over
For each mortal soul.
When life race is done,
Will I reach right goal?

And how have I passed
Through this life, spent my time?
On cleaning and flossing
And making up rhyme?

How much time in worship?
How much time in prayer?
Doing Your pleasure,
Your presence aware?

When I relax,
From my day I unwind,
What does that look like?
What's my leisure time?

When do I snuggle
To hide in my heart
Your Word and promise?
When does worship start?

Am I found praising
As I open my eyes?
How start my day?
Thoughts are time's prize.

Where do I focus
Today's energy?
Jesus or stuff . . .
Which one sets free?

I AM with You

So I bring captive
My thoughts to this time.
Early each morning
I choose You as mine.

And then through the day
Spirit keeps me on point:
Time spent in worship
Your Presence anoints.

And so it is noticed
By others I meet
I'm different when I've
Spent my time at Your feet.

And I've received manna,
Enough for the day.
When I'm jealous for God,
Put You first in this way.

Then dying to self's
Not so hard as I go
Doing Your purpose,
Reflecting Your glow.

It's much less important
That all things get done
Than spending my time
Loving God, Spirit, Son.

Am I jealous for You, God?
You are jealous for me.

Karen J Chisholm

Great Things

God, You have done great things for me.
Provided well; I rejoice in Thee.

Excellent Your works, Your deeds,
Your glory and Your fame.
I cry out and shout to heaven:
"Exalted is Your name!"

God, You're my salvation;
I will trust, not be afraid.
In Christ I am forgiven;
At the cross my fears are laid.

With joy I'm drawing water
Out of wells of life salvation.
You're my strength and song of trust
I sing to every nation.

You've done excellent things, O Lord,
Well known through all the earth.
And now You've sent Your Son who gave
His life for our new birth.

And if His gift of life to us
Then wasn't yet enough,
He sent us Holy Spirit,
Glorious gift from heaven above.

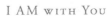

Holy is the Lord!
Mighty is His name!
Every tongue and nation shout!
Everywhere proclaim:

God is great! God is good!
God is glorified!
Jesus Christ is Lord of all.
In Him I abide.
Amen

Karen J Chisholm

Being Fully Present

Lord, how is my attitude?
Is my heart a servant's heart?
When did I reach out to one,
Esteem them better, do my part?

Was my attitude correct then?
Did I lay my own plans down?
Taking time to focus on them
So they knew without a sound

They had my attention?

None of all the multitasking
Builds relationships and trust.
One-on-one and head-to-head
And heart-to-heart I must

Listen slowly, see more clearly,
Hear their words and watch each face
Get their meaning, comprehending,
Giving self no thought or place.

They'll feel understood.

Can I listen without thinking,
Without application then?
If I put myself aside,
Can I make it about them?

This is my gift in relation:
No agenda. Just to be.
They feel heard, could be the first time.
I gain something too, I see.

They are valued more.

Such a long time I have lived
And only now this simple truth:
Lose your life, be spent on others.
Then they'll listen. Here's the proof.

If there's someone who will listen,
Without judging let me talk,
I feel closer, want to know them,
Close beside them want to walk.

I'm accepted here.

So I see now just what You did,
Do today if truth be told.
Christ, You're my belov'd example.
I will follow in Your mold.

Deny self, take up my cross,
And walk more closely by Your side,
Give myself to You today
As I will serve and You will guide.

We will walk as One.

Karen J Chisholm

Walk in the Light

I said I wouldn't do it again, but I did.
I said I wouldn't go there,
Wouldn't eat that,
Wouldn't say it,
But I stand here in my guilt.

O wretched woman that I am,
What I would not do, I do, like Paul.
What I would not say is said,
And only later do I see my failure.

Walk in the Light. I'm trying.
Hold to Your hand. I forget.

Speak Your Word, say Your name;
Spirit sword lies there dusty
And my faith is real rusty.

But deep down inside I know
I can tell You all.
You – only You – can be trusted.
Even myself I betray.

You stand here waiting
Ever beside me,
Bidding me call on Your Name.
For there is the power I'm lacking,
There is the strength that I seek.
When my attention is taken by other,
I forget One who is meek.

I AM with You

Every triumph You've applauded.
Every breakthrough You have cheered.
All I have needed, recognized, heeded,
Each, every blessing You've steered.

Why do I take You for granted?
Wait for hard trial to call?
Each breath is measured
Each triumph treasured
You are here with me through all.

I need only to breathe Your Name
And peace reigns all throughout my soul.
I smile as my burden is lifted,
Then laugh at my wrinkles: life's toll.

Why do I forget You so easily?
Why do dark thoughts hold my mind?

Even a child
Told repeatedly they're beautiful
Still thinks they're ugly.
Who planted that lie?

What is this blight on our soul?
Born in a world sold to sin,
Slave to the darkness within.
Light of salvation our rescue.
Why then we fall back?
Habits reclaim, wrack?
So once again we call on You!

Karen J Chisholm

Teach us to walk in the Light.
Spirit, bring breakthrough again.
Remind of Redeemer
'Til our mind is cleaner
As we seek, then cling close to Him.

I am a child of the King.
I can do all things through Christ.

Every word spoken I turn to His face,
Seeking more closely walk in His embrace,
Start each day holding His hand full of grace.
Choosing each moment to focus on Him,
I begin winning this battle I'm in,
And I'm ready to take up my cross and go on.

It's just another day, but I'm warm.
'Cause I'm walking in the Light of Your Presence.
Again.

Breakthrough!

Lord, I get discouraged
When things don't go my way.
Yesterday I was able and sure.
I'm not so strong today.

The sky's the same, the sun still shines
But inside, I'm blue and gray.
I know You're here, You calm my fear
I know I'm near a breakthrough!

When all I've sought and all I've planned
And all I've done combine,
My efforts only count for Christ
When Your will they align.

And when I bow my head in prayer
And humble myself low,
You work through me, my praise is free,
You bring to me a breakthrough!

New life breaks forth inside my heart,
My Spirit soars in joy.
My soul, reborn, cries "Abba!"
My lips Your songs employ.

I rise to meet the day again.
Love brims in me anew
Then overflows in prayer of thanks,
All honor I give You.

Karen J Chisholm

Breakthrough! Breakthrough!
The promises turn real!
Breakthrough! Breakthrough!
No need contain my zeal!

You keep Your promise and Your Word,
Supply my every need.
And all You ask: stick to the task,
Christ's love the only creed.

I'm stronger now. I've broken through;
I turn to lend a hand.
Reaching to those coming too,
I help others to stand.

Together forth to win the fight,
To set yet others free,
As soldiers in Your army sure,
Obey our Lord's decree

By helping others who are down,
Have fallen, feel remorse,
Encourage them by reaching out,
Pray with them through life course.

All of us together praying
Strengthens every one.
Comforted, we comfort others,
Following Your Son

To breakthrough!

No Condemnation

I see my faults, Lord; You see my value.
I see what's wrong; You see what's right.
I see my would've, could've, should've;
You see nothing but my light
And smile.

There is no condemnation
To those who are in Christ,
For we are free to walk in liberty
You sent your Son to pay sin's price
In Your Spirit we are free

No condemnation. You see complete.
By Your Word, I will believe,
I keep my mind on You,
And follow Spirit's lead,
Accept me as I am,
And trust that You are pleased

Because Your word says
The law's requirement
Christ fulfilled in me
I am free.

Karen J Chisholm

No condemnation!
I am in Christ!
He is my Lord!
My very life!
And I am free to just be me!

Not to be perfect
But to let Jesus
Be perfect for me.
I can love.

I AM with You

How Will I Know It's You?

I need You, Lord; I'm at a crossroads.
What is Your will for me?
How can I know that I will please You?
It's Your face I long to see.

With life choices, I need to know:
How will it all turn out?
I don't want to choose the wrong road,
Wrong mate, wrong church, in doubt.

I'm not feeling You close by me;
No obvious answer awaits.
I'm pressing in to You and trusting;
Is this a test of faith?

I seek in earnest here in my Bible;
I'm praying and listening too.
Give me a hint, grant me direction,
And please let me know it's You.

I'll take a step;
I trust that You'll guide.
When You open doors;
I'll go inside.

My doubt comes from me.
I don't know what I'm doing,
But I trust You to lead.

Karen J Chisholm

Perceiving

You are not revealed to sight,
So we do not see.
We're convinced things brought to light
Are only things that be.

You designed all that is;
We see only some.
Seeing microscopically,
We've only begun.

If we choose to shun our doubts,
Choose belief instead,
By faith to seek You with our hearts,
Believe not by our head,

You make sure we understand
You're *with* us on this plane.
We commence to comprehend,
Awakened spirit train.

We begin perceiving.

We begin to walk in Light,
See revealed new world.
Looking now with spirit sight
At hidden things unfurled.

I AM with You

All seems new and wonderful,
Each cloud and flower and tree.
Then 'come aware by Spirit pull,
You're here with us indeed.

How did spirit come alive
In us in this new way?
Changed from stupor now to thrive
On every word You say?

There is but one way to Father:
Strait gate by Your Son.
Born again, new son and daughter
Spirit life begun.

We are now perceiving.

Jesus is the way, the truth,
The life we weren't aware.
Believing brings the unseen proof
We learn to cast each care.

Our spirit hungry for God's Word,
Your will revealed to man,
Faith grows by the Word we've heard
As You show us Your plan.

We learn of Adam and the Fall,
Of Eve and serpent's guile.
How sold in sin, held in its thrall,
Mankind lived a long while.

Karen J Chisholm

Fulness of time long prophesied
Brought babe in manger here.
Your only Son came to this side
And God to man drew near.

Yet few were then perceiving.

God's Son, Jesus, trained twelve men,
Had women followers too.
Words of life flowed freely then,
Yet He revealed hard truth.

Aware of all, spoke Father's words;
He knew His fate foretold.
Fulfilled the law, did what He heard,
Obeyed to death: cross cold.

Laid in the tomb two days in death,
Took up His life the third
Was seen of men whose bated breath
From grief to joy transferred.

Sent the promise of the Father
When ten days they'd prayed.
Holy Spirit to empower, they
Boldly preached that day.

Men truth began perceiving.

I AM with You

Though Son to Father had returned,
The Comforter had come.
Three thousand new believers burned
To tell of risen Son.

Then You scattered; new believers
Who took the Good News out.
They became Your soul retrievers,
Fishers of men, no doubt.

These men turned world upside down,
Old ways of thinking changed.
Planted churches many towns,
Broke off spiritual chains.

Jesus' words repeated oft
With letters written then
Became New Testament of God,
Your Word come down to men.

When men began perceiving,
God sons began receiving.

Karen J Chisholm

My Offering

Lord, I love You, want to know You.
Want to worship You more and more.
I long to please You, yet I falter.
Imperfect offering. I need restored.

Keep me by You, hid within You,
Only Jesus can then be seen.
Lord, Your blood is all sufficient;
Make my life be new and clean.

Take my heart, Lord, given freely.
Take my hands, my feet, my voice.
Use my life, my days, my hours to
Help someone make you their choice.

Only holy I know You are
Righteous, True, redeeming man.
In You, Lord, I can do all things
My life offering for your plan.

All above, below, beyond
Your throne, footstool, stars' glory song,
All bow to You, their God and King.
I, too, offer everything.

Holy, Holy, Holy Lord
Saints and angels well-adored
Accept my praise, my offering
My God, my Savior, and my King.

Alleluia! Alleluia!
Alleluia! Amen!

I AM with You

Awesome

Awesome. Just awesome.
Precious, Holy God.
Delightful, so delightful
To know Your written word
Humbling, very humbling
To know Your own regard.

Worthy, You are worthy
To be worshipped and adored.
Holy, O so Holy
You are Holy, Risen Lord.

Jesus, Glorious Savior,
Meek and humble as a man
Risen, You are risen
King of Kings, yet God's own Lamb

Mystery, Revealed Mystery
Heaven's Purpose: Father's Plan
Salvation, forever pardoned
From sin: the fall of man.

Karen J Chisholm

Jesus, Son of Man
While Son of God
Humbled and submitted
In obedience walked this earth's sod
Glorious in Your Kingdom now
Seated at right hand of God
Coming soon in glory
Seen of men
As Son of God

Heaven to earth
Then earth to Glory
Coming back,
You'll end earth's story
All made new,
Redeemed, we'll stand
Worship loved, forever planned
Holy
Kingdom
Of God
Glory! Glory!
Hallelujah!
Amen!

Holy, Yet...

Lord, You are amazing:
Holy, yet approachable.
God Eternal, Massive Being,
Awesome Energy.

Creator, not created;
You have always been
Holy, Awesome, Uncontained,
Yet live inside of men.

Glory all is Yours;
It is who You are.
Yet You choose us, mortal men,
To dwell with from afar.

If we will but allow,
Closer You will draw.
Man alone can make this choice:
To worship, keep Your Law.

And if we look real close,
In seeking, we will find.
The way to You brings blessings true,
We learn You're more than kind.

You're Holy, yet approachable.
Holy, yet care more.
Welcome seekers' messy tries
With blessings from great store.

Karen J Chisholm

Who can hope to know You?
Your vastness unexplained.
You take us as we come to You
And love us just the same
As if
WE
Were holy.

Holy, yet unmeasured Love
Prepared the perfect Lamb
Part of You and part of us,
Your Son, yet Son of Man.

You required sacrifice
Of worship with life blood
Of bull and sheep and bird You chose,
Of oil and flour good.

And made a way for sinning ones
To cover marring stains
In order to be clean enough
That living would remain.

And all the law's requirements
Shadowed from afar
The Gift You planned for lowly man
With herald and with star.

So Light of Heaven, in Your time,
Became a man with skin.
Your only Son, Your Sacrifice,
Who full atoned for sin.

I AM with You

Holy, yet approachable,
He called, "Come follow me."
And those who followed witnessed more
Of life with One in Three.

Agape added Holy Word,
Unknown commandments came:
Love yourself, love others more,
And cease affixing blame.

"Too hard!" some cried. "Impossible!"
Unfazed, Your Son kept on
Completing all was called to do,
Laid down His life and won

New life for whosoever
Would believe and choose death too,
Denying self, take up the cross
And serve The Way, The Truth.

For as He took His own life back,
He conquered death and grave,
Paraded them in conq'ring chains
While gifts to men He gave.

And though this happened long ago,
He isn't bound by time.
So you and I today can choose,
Believe, and join the climb.

Karen J Chisholm

Daily dying to ourselves
His life in us proclaims
Whosoever will may come;
He's not concerned with stains.

Come any who would be redeemed
From hopelessness within
And be reborn, breaking all chains
That kept us bound in sin.

New life in Christ, true miracle,
His blood avails forever
To bring new hope to hopeless ones
Sin's hold o'er us to sever.

He's gone, preparing place for us
Who serve and follow peace,
And we will join Him when all trials
That shape us finally cease.

Look up!
Redemption draweth nigh.

Section III

ME SPEAKING TO OTHERS

Fear

Where does it come from?
This feeling that flits in and out,
Hiding in our days and peopling our nights . . .

Is it from inside ourselves,
A legacy of the dim past?
A part of us intrinsically . . .
Or invited in a weak moment?

Can another wish it on us?
Give it away? Contaminate us?

Or do we draw it to us, hold it close,
And pet it as if it were an old, familiar friend?
Who is it? Why does it feel

As though it is a part of ourselves,
A mirror of our secret thoughts,
But never our wishes?

Why do we identify with it so closely,
Guard the knowledge of it so securely,
Hide it as though it wasn't there?
If we don't tell anyone, maybe it isn't.

Maybe it will go away.

Maybe.

*For God hath not given us a spirit of fear;
but of power, and of love, and of a sound mind.*
II Timothy 1:7

Music!

I am thankful, thankful, thankful for music!
Lyrics and melodies, stories in rhyme,
Worship our Father, waltz or cut time.

I love music! It reaches my heart.
It gives me a voice and can make the tears start.

I'm happy or sad. I'm good or I'm bad.
I can tell how I feel and can pour out my heart,
Next moment invincible or funny or smart.

Music unlocks all we have deep inside.
With music I've shouted and
Danced, laughed, and cried.

I'm thankful for music and give praise to Him!
Forever I'll worship, for I've entered in
To places where David, Paul, Moses have been.

I seek Him myself, and He lets me find
Treasures He's hidden for just me in time.

Lord, I give praise, glory, honor to Thee.
God is good. All the time.
By the Blood we're set free
To speak and to worship, to sing and to pray.

To Yahweh and Jesus we give all our praise
In slow, pensive meter or hard, pounding ways.

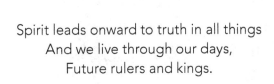

I AM with You

Spirit leads onward to truth in all things
And we live through our days,
Future rulers and kings.

Pressing on to the mark of high calling in Christ,
We run, walk, or stumble –
Low self-esteem or with feist.

He takes our best effort, intentions, and plans,
Then makes us acceptable by
Blood from His hands.

And all of my effort, my offering, my work
Is used building His Kingdom right here on earth.

And I know I'm a part of the family of God,
Seen holy in heaven while walking this sod.

But by His mercy, His love, and His grace.
We are invited believe, seek His face.

And it all can be told in waltz or in swing,
In foxtrot or limbo; expressing, I sing:
Jesus loves me. This I know. I'm thankful.

Ragged meter? No matter.
Forget to close rhyme?
It's all little consequence;
Doting Father thinks it's fine.

For I am accepted and wanted and loved.
All my efforts are praised and valued above.
And my Father says to me:
I love you, love you, love you.
Love you, love you, LOVE YOU . . .

KAREN J CHISHOLM

My Hand

I look at my hand, intricately formed
Unique of all hands in all time
Resembling the hand of my parent somewhat
Yet solely, remarkably mine.

Considering actions performed every day,
Never thought about, this hand has done
Carries out all my will, each subconscious command
As a servant, it compares to none.

Today in my Bible I read, "I the Lord
Thy God will hold thy right hand . . .
Fear not, I will help thee" and I am amazed
This appendage is part of God's Plan!?!

He holds my right hand and helping me there,
He's the power through my hand to get wealth,
To reach out through me touching lives for their good
Or for ill if I'm out for myself.

With this hand held open, I give others help
Or closed in a fist, I refuse.
But when I step back and consider it's held
By God's hand, then I know I must choose.

"Choose ye this day whom ye will serve"
Joshua words echo through time.
The deeper choice is: Will I choose life or death?
Whose hand will hold mine through life's climb?

I AM with You

Darkness or light? Wrong or right?
Who knows what risks lie ahead?
I'm given choice free: serve others or me.
Comes to trust, can't do that if I'm dead.

So who is my God? I have one for sure.
If I think I'm in charge, I'm deceived.
This hand serves either the wicked or just
Right here, my heart is the key.

"I'm not a servant! A lackey despised!
I have importance. I'm free!
Who are you then to speak to me thus?
My life belongs to just me!"

Oh, really?
You don't even meet your own needs.
Consider that none stands alone.
You buy or you sell or you barter each day
To acquire or take care what you own.

A salesman you are,
Have been one since your birth.
A good one gets all his needs met.
Loud infant for milk or sweet talking for love,
It's giving you must do to get.

So now I look down. At the end of my arm
Is the servant that started this say.
This hand, held firm by the God that I serve,
The One in my heart today.

Karen J Chisholm

The Same Man

I met a young woman the other day,
It seemed that the meeting was planned.
She spoke of her love in a familiar way,
I think we're married to the same man!

I watched her glow as she shared her joy.
How animated her hands . . .
As she spoke lovingly of this golden boy.
I think we're married to the same man!

Her heart was with him,
Seemed to ponder his grace
As her voice was brimming
With the glow of her stand.
And I too felt giddy, remembering his embrace!
I think we're married to the same man!

He's amazing and wonderful and cherishes dear.
If share him I must, I'm determined I can,
I cannot part from him; on this point I'm clear.
I know now we're married to the same man.

So we'll join in and share in our loving affiliation
With this man who transforms, evincing his plan.
We'll unite our lives together in his adoration.
I'm happy we're married to the same man . . .

. . . Jesus.

I AM with You

Trust

Trust is learned and earned and broken,
A commodity expected at first.
Then time reveals motives unspoken,
Revealing a blessing or curse.

Relational duties attended or shirked
Build or tear down over time.
Strong, loving feelings maintained with hard work
Satisfy both who say "mine."

Trust is a concept unknown to the hurt,
Ones who weren't given a choice.
Neglected, abused, tossed in the dirt,
Never allowed their own voice.

Trust once betrayed loses its strength,
Relational choosing of sides.
Cover, protect, at any length,
Walls of suspicion abide.

Trust in a God who constantly loves
Is hard for those living with care.
But patient He waits in His kingdom above
'Til we realize He's always there.

And choose . . . to trust.

Karen J Chisholm

Forgive Me

Days and weeks and months go by.
Sometimes I laugh, sometimes I cry,
But deep, deep down inside of me,
My spirit cries to be set free.

A wrong was done, then hid in shame
And now things just are not the same
Between the one I love and me
Whose spirit too must be set free.

I sought to say it's not my fault;
I did it out of love – I thought.
But time and grace have shown to me
What my pride wouldn't let me see.

In darkness it grew worse and worse,
Then my rebellion brought a curse
'Til God's Holy Spirit convicted me
And lit the way to be set free.

The love of God, the light of life
Shown on that situation there
Dispelled the darkness hiding what
I had covered with my fear.

For what I thought or what I felt
Wasn't really that important.
It's what God thought or what God felt
That struck this somber note discordant.

I AM with You

I was wrong, Lord, to play God
When You already had control.
Father, I ask Your forgiveness;
Blood of Jesus, cleanse my soul.

Sister, I know I'm forgiven,
God still loves me just the same.
But you and I are left with wounds and
I'm the one who takes the blame.

Sister, love is what you gave me,
But I chose to hear a lie.
A half-truth, really, but a "no truth"
Is more obvious to the eye.

What I'm asking is, forgive me.
I was wrong and you were right.
Love covers a multitude of sins.
That's the love that sets wrongs right.

Sister, we would find no fault if
I were perfect and you were too,
But God is working to perfect us.
Let's love each other 'til God is through.

Karen J Chisholm

The Peace of God

The peace of God transcends the mind.
It comes by giving in,
Releasing all you've left behind,
And trusting it to Him.

Over all, He hovers near;
Any one may call,
Leaving off all doubt and fear,
Giving to Him all.

Every moment we can rest;
Trusting, we abide.
When we face the next life test,
He is at our side.

When we thought we were alone
In tests gone through before,
He was with us then unknown,
Knocking at heart's door.

Looking back through eyes of faith
We see He's ever been
Keeping us by loving grace,
Drawing us to Him.

I AM with You

And thus we know He understands.
He loves us though we're sinners.
Sore trials, failures, struggles, and
Weak moments come to winners.

It does not yet appear what we
Will be like when He comes,
But we can trust that we will be
Just like Him: God the Son.

And so in His peace we abide,
Our own peace doesn't stay.
Yet He is ever at our side,
His peace is ours today.

As we, thankful, just take time
To pray, give burden o'er,
His peace settles, we unwind,
Let go worry; adore.

And praise comes ready to our lips
For Holy One above.
Thankful, saved from this life's slips,
Oasis rest: His Love.

And so, deep breath followed by sigh
Signals burden down,
Leaving to the One drawn nigh
All worry, every frown.

Traded so unequally
For Peace of God, we find
His Joy floods; we're lighter, free,
At peace our troubled mind.

And strength redounds as hope and light
Flood us with energy
To live another day and fight
Through trials 'til we're free.

To live
In peace.

Wishes

If wishes were horses . . .
                . . . Ah, but they're not.
Wispy and dreamy and fluffy, more like.
Made up of glory we hope to attain, but
Won't reach for, aspire to, believe in, or claim.

Wishes are shadows or glimpses perhaps.
They're daydreams and gold things
    And wants wearing hats
Of gossamer cloud-mist, of vapor or light,
Elusive, seductive, seem real, lost to sight.

Let them go or call them back?
No, don't bother, there are more.
Shall I catch them? Shall I find them?
No, of course not. Whatever for?

Don't you want them? Aren't they yours then?
Too much work and too much pain.
I never was cut out for suffering.
Too much toil, too little gain.

Would you rather live on wishes?
Ne'er to live, to die the same?
Days and nights becoming years then,
What to show for? Who to blame?

Yes, I see then, I must choose then
Whom I'll serve now, where I'll dwell.
Set before me life and death then
Let me choose 'tween heav'n and hell.

Like the beggar, like the rich man,
Trouble, toil, or life of ease.
Let me work now for the Master
Suffer, pray, give, humble, please.

For He loved me, died to show me,
Let me know His plan foretold,
Gave me His love; now I love Him,
Like the prophets, men of old.

Then, in dying, He will raise me.
I with Him will rule o'er much.
For in life I chose to love Him,
Died to self, of Kingdom such.

If wishes were horses . . .
                . . . I'd rather walk.

Section IV

AUTHOR

About the Author

Karen J Chisholm loves the Lord and these poems and writings come from her early morning quiet time with God.

She lives in Texas, in the Greater Houston area; is a published pianist, singer, songwriter; is Director of Music Ministries at her local church; and is retired from working in the U.S. Space Program.

Karen has three sons, six grandchildren, and *many* others who refer to her as "Grandma Karen."

Her interests are singing and playing music; reading; writing Christian music, stories, and poetry; home cooking; and playing games.

Karen's heart is worshipping the Lord in song and with others, but she also enjoys "doing music" with other musicians. About once a month, you will find her singing, playing piano, and acting silly at a local assisted living residence with Doc Pepper in their duo called *Rigol* (which is almost French for almost funny). Karen leads a group from her church called *Joyful Noise Praise Team and Nickel Strings* in bringing gospel music and old hymns to the senior citizens in the Greater Houston area. She often refers to Joyful Noise as being "*famous!* . . . in Baytown, Crosby, Channelview, Highlands, LaPorte, and Deer Park."

Karen's first CD, *I Delight in You* (which can be found on YouTube) released in 2013 and recorded at The Vault Recording Studios in Houston, Texas, showcases twelve of the more than 300 songs God has inspired her to write. She performs these, along with hymns and Southern Gospel songs in her church and its community, and at other churches by request.

Printed in the USA
CPSIA information can be obtained
at www.ICGtesting.com
LVHW031249071023
760211LV00009B/1076